Wildly Weird Weather

That's a moonbow!

By Kristen Rajczak Nelson

Please visit our website, www.garethstevens.com. For a free color catalog of all our high-quality books, call toll free 1-800-542-2595 or fax 1-877-542-2596.

Cataloging-in-Publication Data

Names: Rajczak Nelson, Kristen.
Title: That's a moonbow! / Kristen Rajczak Nelson.
Description: New York : Gareth Stevens Publishing, 2024. | Series: Wildly weird weather | Includes glossary and index.
Identifiers: ISBN 9781538288030 (pbk.) | ISBN 9781538288047 (library bound) | ISBN 9781538288054 (ebook)
Subjects: LCSH: Moonbows–Juvenile literature.
Classification: LCC QC976.M66 R35 2024 | DDC 551.56'7–dc23

First Edition

Published in 2024 by
Gareth Stevens Publishing
2544 Clinton St.
Buffalo, NY 14224

Designer: Corinne Eberwine
Editor: Theresa Emminizer

Photo credits: Cover, Jan Kroupa photography/Shutterstock.com; p. 5 (rainbow) S.Borisov/Shutterstock.com; p. 5 (moonbow) Francisco Llano Tome/Shutterstock.com; p. 6 Mila Drumeva/Shutterstock.com; p. 6 (inset) VectorMine/Shutterstock.com; p. 9 Phillip B. Espinasse/Shutterstock.com; p. 10 Roman Mikhailiuk/Shutterstock.com; p. 12 Panos Karas/Shutterstock.com; p. 13 james_stone76/Shutterstock.com; p. 14 KITAMU/Shutterstock.com; p. 17 Pyngodan/Shutterstock.com; p. 19 kdshutterman/Shutterstock.com; p. 21 KES47/Wikimedia.com.

Some of the images in this book illustrate individuals who are models. The depictions do not imply actual situations or events.

Printed in the United States of America

CPSIA compliance information: Batch #CS24GS: For further information contact Gareth Stevens, New York, New York at 1-800-542-2595.

Find us on

Contents

Words in the glossary appear in **bold** type the first time they are used in the text.

Color in the Sky

Seeing a rainbow feels magical! It's such a treat to see the beautiful colors across the sky when the sun comes out after a long rainy day.

Imagine seeing something just as special but at night! This may seem impossible. In order for a rainbow to be seen, the sun must be out. However, a lunar rainbow, or moonbow, occurs by the light of the moon! Both **phenomena** happen because of how light moves through the water in

That's a Fact!

The word lunar means having to do with the moon.

rainbow

moonbow

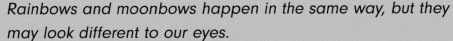

^ *Rainbows and moonbows happen in the same way, but they may look different to our eyes.*

radio waves   microwaves   infrared   visible light   ultraviolet   X-rays   gamma waves

That's a Fact!

Humans can only see some kinds of light.
What we can see is called visible light.

wavelength. Violet, or purple, has the shortest. The other colors are somewhere in between.

To human eyes, light—such as sunlight—looks white. All the light waves are moving together through the air. At times, light can be separated into the whole **spectrum** of colors.

< *This piece of glass is called a prism. It has many flat sides, or faces. When white light shines through a prism, it's separated into all the colors of the rainbow!*

Light Through Water

A rainbow occurs when sunlight enters a drop of water. The light waves slow down because the water is **denser** than the air around it. The light waves bend, or refract, as they enter the drop of water. Each light wave bends a different amount.

That's a Fact!

In order for a rainbow to form, sunlight has to enter the raindrop at just the right **angle**. That's why we don't see rainbows every time it rains.

The light is **reflected** on the inside of the drop of water.

It speeds up a bit and bends again as it leaves the raindrop.

The light has separated into its different wavelengths.

We see a rainbow!

∧ *This rainbow looks like the shape of an arc, or half circle. A full rainbow is a whole circle! Only people in airplanes in the right place at the right time might see this from above.*

Double rainbows, or secondary rainbows, happen when light is reflected twice inside a drop of water.

The Right Time and Place

In order to see a rainbow, the conditions must be right. The person seeing the rainbow must have their back to the sun. There needs to be water in the atmosphere, so it must be raining, have just stopped raining, or be **foggy**. Finally, the sun needs to be low in the sky. Rainbows are most common in the late afternoon because of this.

Moonbows only form under certain conditions too! They happen in much the same way as rainbows.

That's a Fact!

Rainbows are more common in summer than winter.

Sunlight, Moonlight

Moonbows happen when moonlight enters drops of water in the atmosphere. Just as it does when a rainbow forms, the light refracts, reflects within the drop, and refracts again. The light waves separate into colors by wavelength as they leave the drop.

Aristotle

That's a Fact!

Greek thinker Aristotle was the first to write about moonbows in about 350 BCE.

But there's still some mystery about how moonbows form. Where does the light for a moonbow come from if it happens at night?

The moon doesn't make its own light. Moonlight is light from the sun reflecting off the moon's surface!

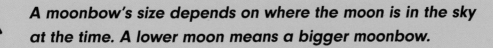

∧ *A moonbow's size depends on where the moon is in the sky at the time. A lower moon means a bigger moonbow.*

Whether they look white or colorful, all moonbows will look dimmer than rainbows. **^**

Is It White?

Rainbows can be **faint** in the sky or have very bold colors. No matter how dark the colors look though, when you see a rainbow, there's no question it's made up of colors. Moonbows, on the other hand, most often look white to the human eye!

Scientists know for sure that moonbows have colors. Certain kinds of **photographs** show all the colors found in a moonbow. Some lucky viewers have seen a colorful moonbow too.

That's a Fact!

The sun is about 400,000 times brighter than the light from a full moon! That's why a rainbow's colors show up better than a moonbow's.

Majestic Moonbows

It's possible to see a moonbow while looking at the stars near your home on a rainy or foggy night. But that's not the only place you might see a moonbow!

Waterfalls create **mist** as the water falls over rock. This mist may be enough to create a moonbow as the moon glows above. Spray from the ocean can also give off the water needed for a moonbow to form. What delightful places to spot moonbows!

Victoria Falls is between the African countries of Zambia and Zimbabwe. It's a well-known spot to see moonbows. >

That's a Fact!

The state park where Cumberland Falls is found in Kentucky puts out a **schedule** of when it's likely visitors can see a moonbow over the waterfall!

Halo or Bow?

Like rainbows, moonbows are most often going to look like arcs to the human eye. Sometimes, the moon looks like it's ringed by a circle of light. This is called a lunar halo. It's a lot like a moonbow!

Lunar halos occur when moonlight reflects and refracts within ice crystals in some kinds of clouds. The halos often have a bit of red on the inside of the circle. They may have a violet edge on the outside.

In the past, people believed a ring around the moon—a lunar halo—meant bad weather was coming. >

That's a Fact!

Halos appear around the sun too. Never look straight at the sun, however. You could hurt your eyes.

See a Moonbow!

Moonbows aren't seen very often. The conditions need to be just right! As you've read, there must be water in the air from rain, fog, or mist. Then, a moonbow is more likely to appear during a full or nearly full moon. The sky needs to be clear with few to no clouds.

Finally, someone looking for a moonbow needs to have their back to the moon. The best time to look is a few hours after sunset or before sunrise.

All it takes to make a moonbow is water and moonlight—as well as the right conditions!

It needs to be very dark to see a moonbow. Any lights from houses or cars can hide a dim moonbow.

drop of water

moonlight

How a Moonbow Forms

reflection

refraction

Glossary

angle: The space or shape that forms when two lines meet.

atmosphere: The mixture of gases that surround a planet.

dense: Packed very closely together.

faint: Not clearly seen.

foggy: Having fog, or many small drops of water floating in the air.

mist: Very small drops of water in the air, often from rain or rising from a body of water.

phenomenon: A fact or event that is observed.

photograph: A picture made with a camera.

reflect: To give back light.

schedule: A list of when some things will happen.

spectrum: The colors that a ray of light may be separated into, including red, orange, yellow, green, blue, indigo, and violet.

wavelength: The distance from one wave of energy to another as it travels from point to point.

For More Information

Books

Gunasekara, Mignonne. *Experiments with Light.* New York, NY: KidHaven Publishing, 2022.

Vail, Grace. *More Freaky Weather Stories.* New York, NY: Gareth Stevens Publishing, 2020.

Websites

What Causes a Rainbow?
scijinks.gov/rainbow/
Read up on why rainbows appear here.

What Is a Moonbow?
www.sciencefocus.com/planet-earth/moonbows-8-stunning-photos-of-the-rare-night-sky-phenomenon/
Check out recent photos of moonbows!

Index